BIG CATS

Of all cats, the lion is the most social (*top and opposite, bottom right*). The nucleus of a lion pride is a group of between two and nine related females, who defend a common territory. Members of a pride do not always stay together, but frequently split up into smaller sub-prides.

Two or more females within a pride may give birth to cubs simultaneously, the different mothers freely suckling each other's cubs. It is not unusual to see two or three litters of cubs together (*opposite, centre and top right*). Lionesses remain with the pride

By roaring, male lions make known their presence to other males, warning them that the territory is inhabited. A similar message is conveyed by spray-urinating against the bushes in their territory (*opposite, bottom right*).

they are born into, but males are evicted from their natal prides around the age of two-and-a-half years. They then form nomadic groups and, at about four years old, are ready to challenge other males for the possession of a territory. This results in aggressive struggles for dominance which frequently lead to injury or death. Those that manage to displace the existing males from a territory establish a coalition of male lions and gain mating rights to the females. If the females have cubs from a former union, they will not be receptive to new mates who will often kill the cubs or severely wound them, leaving them to die (*top left*). This brings the females on heat and the new males are able to sire (*opposite, bottom left*) and protect their own cubs, rather than the offspring of other male lions.

Africa's largest and most inspiring carnivore, the lion, is the dominant predator in most savanna ecosystems (*left*). Fifteen thousand years ago the lion was widely distributed in Europe, and today is still found in the Middle East and as far as northern India. On the African continent, the lion has been eradicated from much of its former range and is now mainly confined to the larger game reserves.

Although it is known to feed on virtually every mammal, the lion's principle food consists of mammals in the 100–300 kg mass range, including gemsbok, wildebeest, hartebeest and zebra. Like all carnivores, lions are opportunists and will exploit any potential food supply, as seen by this attempt to extract a tortoise from its shell (*opposite, top*). They are also known to tackle porcupines. However, the porcupine's sharp quills provide

a good defence, and sometimes it is safer just to look (*right*)! Lions hunt predominantly under cover of darkness, and typically stalk their prey before a short chase of between 100 m and 200 m ensues. During the hunt, co-operation between lions may be high, particularly in open habitats. They do not consciously use wind direction when hunting but their chance of success is higher if they are downwind from their prey. The male lion does far more hunting than was previously believed to be the case, and spends a great deal of time away from the company of females. The cubs are permitted to feed on the kill only once the adults have had their fill (*opposite, centre*).

Lions, like nearly all carnivores, are able to survive indefinitely without water, obtaining liquid from the meat and blood of the prey that they capture (*opposite, top*).
Overleaf: Lion and lioness pair

Big Cats and Other African Predators

The leopard represents the typical cat: solitary, beautiful, aloof (*opposite, left*) and lightning fast to pounce when the moment is right (*above*). It has a wide habitat tolerance, ranging from tropical forests to the fringes of deserts. Long after other large carnivores have been eliminated from an area, the leopard will remain. It is found in the southern parts of the African continent, northwards to the Arabian Peninsula, through the Middle East to the Far East, as far as Siberia and south-eastwards to Sri Lanka and Malaysia.

Leopards are highly secretive and silent (*right below*), and are able to eke out an existence on small animals such as dassies, ground-nesting birds and even mice if larger animals are absent. In protected areas leopards prey on the most common medium-sized antelope such as springbok, impala or reedbuck.

The leopard's habit of dragging its kill into a tree (*opposite, right*) ensures that stronger predators, such as lions and hyaenas, do not rob it of its food. It moves the carcass by straddling it and then, using its powerful neck muscles, will

carry it off to the base of a tree. With a prodigious leap, it claws its way up the tree to the first fork, and if possible will pull it further into the higher branches.

Leopards often compete with cheetahs for prey of the same species. However, competition between the two is reduced by the fact that leopards are mainly nocturnal whereas cheetahs are diurnal – hunting by day.

Male and female leopards hunt in separate territories, the male's territory being the larger and overlapping those of several females. A male will mate with any one of the females whose territories overlap with his own.

Cubs are born in litters of two or three, and are weaned at three months. From about the age of four months, they will accompany their mother on hunts (*opposite, centre*), remaining dependent on her for up to 22 months. Female cubs may inherit part of their mother's territory when they reach breeding age, but the males must move off to seek their own territories elsewhere.

The cheetah is built for speed. Its long and powerful legs, slim body, deep chest, long tail and small head, are all adaptations to permit unexcelled speed (*above*). It is the fastest land mammal and is capable of reaching speeds of up to 95 km per hour. If it fails in its efforts to catch up with its prey after about 400 m at full speed, the cheetah will abandon the hunt as it is likely to suffer organ damage from over-exertion.

In order to gain maximum speed, the cheetah has had to sacrifice a robust skull for a small, streamlined head and for the weakest jaws of a predator its size. This makes killing larger prey more difficult. Small to medium-sized mammals, such as impala, springbok, Thomson's gazelle, steenbok and hares, represent the cheetah's main prey (*left*). After an energetic chase and kill, the cheetah can do little else but lie and pant heavily until it has regained enough strength to begin eating. Since it is the weakest of the larger carnivores, other large predators can easily displace it from its kill.

Although not as agile or as strong as a leopard, the cheetah is able to climb trees and often uses them as a vantage point when looking for prey (*opposite, bottom*), or as a refuge from enemies.

Unlike other large carnivores, the cheetah is diurnal (*centre*). Not only does this reduce competition with the nocturnal predators, but it is essential for the

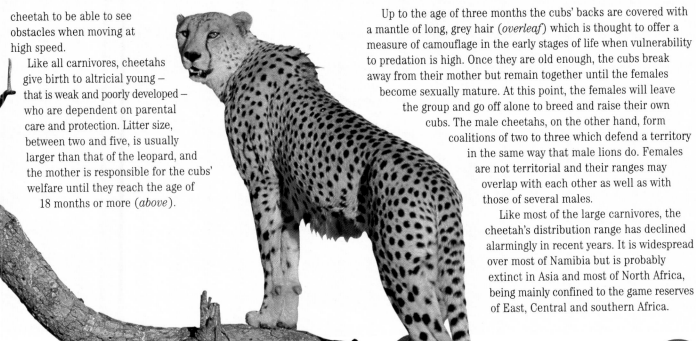

cheetah to be able to see obstacles when moving at high speed.

Like all carnivores, cheetahs give birth to altricial young – that is weak and poorly developed – who are dependent on parental care and protection. Litter size, between two and five, is usually larger than that of the leopard, and the mother is responsible for the cubs' welfare until they reach the age of 18 months or more (*above*).

Up to the age of three months the cubs' backs are covered with a mantle of long, grey hair (*overleaf*) which is thought to offer a measure of camouflage in the early stages of life when vulnerability to predation is high. Once they are old enough, the cubs break away from their mother but remain together until the females become sexually mature. At this point, the females will leave the group and go off alone to breed and raise their own cubs. The male cheetahs, on the other hand, form coalitions of two to three which defend a territory in the same way that male lions do. Females are not territorial and their ranges may overlap with each other as well as with those of several males.

Like most of the large carnivores, the cheetah's distribution range has declined alarmingly in recent years. It is widespread over most of Namibia but is probably extinct in Asia and most of North Africa, being mainly confined to the game reserves of East, Central and southern Africa.

Big Cats and Other African Predators

In Africa, seven species of small, nocturnal, solitary cats are found, but as yet little is known of their behaviour. The caracal is the largest of these (*above and opposite, left*), the male weighing about 15 kg and the female between 10 and 12 kg. This cat is found throughout Africa, except in the true desert regions and the tropical forests; it also occurs in parts of southern Asia. The caracal's diet consists mainly of birds and small mammals, such as springhares and dassies (*above*) but, in spite of its size, it is also able to overcome jackal, wild cat and, in exceptional cases, even prey as large as adult springbok or reedbuck. The caracal is an aggressive animal and has even been known to take over a kill from a group of black-backed jackals. In areas where the black-backed jackal has been eliminated, the caracal is believed to have increased in number and is thought to be a more significant predator of domestic sheep than the jackal.

The long-legged serval (*left below*), weighing about 10 kg, prefers tall grass habitats (*opposite, right*) and vleis, where one of its principal prey species – the vlei rat – is found. Unlike most other cats, it is not averse to hunting in wet, swampy areas.

The African wild cat (*left above*) is an ancestor of the domestic tabby and can easily be mistaken for the latter. Around 6 000 years ago the ancient Egyptians began to domesticate this cat to keep rats and mice out of their granaries. In many of the regions where it is found, it is often the most common of the small carnivores. However, cross-breeding between the domestic cat and the pure African wild cat threatens the species. This cat has a similar habitat tolerance and distribution range to the caracal. Rats and mice comprise its basic diet, but it also eats sun spiders, locusts, birds and small reptiles. African wild cats are known to sit silently near the entrance of a rodent hole, ready to pounce on the occupant as it emerges. They are also good tree climbers and often take refuge in trees when hunted. Some even raise their young in holes found in tree trunks.

The African golden cat occurs from Senegal to Zaïre and Kenya, living in forest and dense scrubland. It preys on small mammals and birds.

The jungle cat inhabits the dry forests and scrub areas of Egypt through to Indochina and Sri Lanka. Its diet is made up of rodents and frogs.

The sand cat, on the other hand, is a desert cat found in North Africa and South West Asia. Rodents, lizards and insects are its main prey.

The smallest cat is the black-footed, or spotted cat, weighing between 1 and 2 kg. It is found only in the arid zones of southern Africa and feeds mainly on rodents, shrews and small birds, but is capable of killing prey larger than itself, such as korhaans and hares.

male lion is present. Spotted hyaenas do, however, obtain most of their food as active and efficient hunters. It is not uncommon for them to kill adult wildebeest and zebra. During the wildebeest calving season, they are the calves' main predators.

Highly social, spotted hyaenas live in clans of up to 100 individuals who co-operate in defending the territory. Females are larger and more dominant than males, having priority over food. Superficially the females' reproductive organs resemble those of the males, giving rise to the misconception that they are hermaphrodites.

The spotted hyaena is a much maligned and misunderstood creature (*top and opposite, bottom*). It is viewed as a cowardly scavenger surviving on the pickings of the more noble carnivores. There is no doubt that hyaenas are efficient scavengers (*opposite, top*); they have the most powerful teeth and jaws in the animal kingdom and are able to crunch up large bones which the other carnivores leave behind. Furthermore, in areas with large numbers of lions, the necessity for hyaenas to hunt is reduced. Since there is plenty of carrion available, they take on a more scavenging role and may drive lions away from their kill, particularly if no large

These animals have an elaborate meeting ceremony (*opposite, bottom*) whereby they stand head to tail, lift the hind leg nearest to the other animal, and sniff and lick each other's erected sexual organs. By exposing their most vulnerable parts to the teeth of another, they display great trust which serves to cement the bond of friendship.

Females give birth to one or two cubs (*opposite, centre*), who are kept in a communal den consisting of narrow tunnels only large enough for the cubs to enter. This provides the cubs with ideal protection when the adults are away. The cubs are born with their eyes open and canine teeth erupted, and may fight fiercely with each other within hours of being born, particularly if they are females. The first-born may sometimes even kill its sibling. Cubs are suckled until a year old, an unusually lengthy suckling period for a carnivore. These nutritional demands on the female account for the small size of the litters and for the large size and dominance of the female who is better able to protect and provide for her young.

The brown hyaena better fits the title of scavenger (*below*) than does the spotted hyaena. The little hunting it does, usually for small prey, is mostly unsuccessful. Killed prey forms an insignificant part of the diet, which more typically consists of mammals hunted by larger carnivores or dead from starvation and disease, as well as wild fruits, insects and ostrich eggs.

Although brown hyaenas forage alone (*bottom left*), they are not solitary like the leopard and will often share a territory. On occasion, two or more females from a clan will share a den which is the social centre of the clan. Like the young of the spotted hyaena, cubs are weaned at the age of one year. From 12 weeks the cubs' milk diet is supplemented with food which the adult members carry to the den. Since the cubs do not depend solely on their mother's milk, the female brown hyaena can raise a larger litter than the spotted hyaena. The female in this species is also not larger than the male, nor does she dominate him.

Brown hyaenas display aggression towards others with the erection of the mane (*top left*). Known as pilo-erection, this occurs when approaching others at a kill or when members of the same sex (but from different groups) meet.

The aardwolf (*above*) is Africa's most specialised carnivore. An aberrant hyaena, it lacks powerful teeth and jaws, and weighs only 9 kg.

It has a discontinuous distribution in Africa, being found only in the south and north-east. In both regions, the aardwolf's diet consists almost entirely of snouted harvester termites.

These animals have developed a large tongue (*right*), adapted for licking up the termites as they forage above the ground. If a foraging termite column is disturbed, the worker termites rush underground and the soldiers emerge, producing distasteful secretions as a form of defence. When the ratio of soldiers to workers reaches a certain level, the aardwolf is repulsed and stops feeding.

It has been calculated that a single aardwolf eats up to 105 million termites in a year, which signifies their considerable importance in controlling the extensive termite populations.

The African wild dog (*opposite, top right*) is one of Africa's most endangered mammals. They are highly social, living in packs which range in size from a pair to as many as 50 individuals. The adult males in the pack are related, as are the females, but the males and females are unrelated.

Normally only the dominant male and female will breed, the female producing a large litter of between 10 and 21 pups. All pack members share in raising the young by regurgitating food to them after hunting (*left*). The pups are weaned around the

age of two months, and at three to five months leave the den with the rest of the pack to take up a nomadic existence (*opposite, bottom*).

Wild dogs hunt early in the morning and in the late afternoon, taking mainly medium-sized prey like impala, wildebeest calves (*below*) and Thomson's gazelles. Although efficient hunters, they do not play havoc with game herds as is often stated. In fact, they will travel large distances to find suitable prey. When a kill is made, adult members allow the pups to eat before feeding themselves (*bottom right*).

Wild dogs show little fear of spotted hyaenas (*opposite, top right*) although, in open environments such as the Serengeti plains, hyaenas often steal their food; they display immense fear of lions who frequently kill both adults and pups. Wild dogs are great roamers, given to straying beyond the confines of protected areas into surrounding farmlands, where they come into conflict with stock farmers.

Besides the African wild dog, there are nine other canids in Africa – four jackals, four true foxes, and one aberrant fox.

The black-backed jackal (*above, left and opposite, top left*) is common over the more arid regions of southern and East Africa. Like all other jackals, this animal is an opportunist, feeding on carrion wherever it is available. However, it is also an efficient hunter of rodents and the young of small and medium-sized antelope (*opposite, top right*). If the opportunity arises it will even attack larger prey who are vulnerable as a result of injury or disease. Reptiles, insects and wild fruits also form part of the black-backed jackal's diet. Male and female pairs are monogamous and defend a specific territory.

The side-striped jackal (*below and opposite, bottom right*) has a white tip to its tail and, at 10 kg, is heavier than the black-backed jackal. It is also seen less often and is more nocturnal. An inhabitant

of the better-watered, higher rainfall areas, it has a wider distribution range than the black-backed jackal. They have a similar diet but the side-striped jackal tends to feed more on vegetable matter.

The golden jackal is found in the arid, short grasslands of East and North Africa, south-east Europe and southern Asia as far east as Burma. On the Serengeti plains the golden jackal whelps during the rainy season when food, in the form of migrating herbivores, is abundant. The black-backed jackal, on the other hand, whelps in the dry season which coincides with a peak in rodent numbers and wild fruits.

With only 400 animals surviving, the Ethiopian wolf, also known as the Simien jackal, is the rarest carnivore in Africa. Threats to its survival include habitat loss and fragmentation, persecution, hybridisation with domestic dogs and disease, particularly rabies. It lives only in afro-alpine habitats, above 3 000 m, where it feeds on the ample rodent community. Ethiopian wolves live in close-knit territorial packs of up to 13 adults. The members forage alone but come together to socialise, patrol and rest at night.

Africa's four foxes are all inhabitants of arid regions. The Cape fox (*below and bottom left*) occurs in southern Africa, whereas the pale fox, Rüppell's fox and the fennec fox occur in North Africa, the latter two also going across into Arabia. They are diminutive, the Cape fox at 4 kg being the largest, and the fennec fox being the smallest at 1 kg. Like all foxes they are adept at catching rodents.

Africa's aberrant fox, the bat-eared fox (*top right and above*), is the only canid to have largely abandoned mammalian prey and to predominantly feed on insects, being particularly partial to harvester termite and beetle larvae. It has more teeth than the other foxes and its large ears are sensitive to the sounds made by insects, even those moving underground. The bat-eared fox occurs in the arid and semi-arid parts of southern and East Africa.

Struik Publishers (Pty) Ltd
(a member of the Struik Publishing Group (Pty) Ltd)
Cornelis Struik House
80 McKenzie Street
Cape Town 8001

Reg. No.: 54/00965/07

First published in 1998

Copyright © 1998 in the published edition:
Struik Publishers (Pty) Ltd
Copyright © 1987, 1994, 1998 text: Gus Mills
Copyright © 1998 photographs: Individual photographers
or their agents as listed below

Designed by Dean Pollard
Edited by Cara Cilliers
Reproduction by Unifoto (Pty) Ltd, Cape Town
Repro Coordinator: Andrew de Kock
Printed by CTP Book Printers, Parow

ISBN 1 86825 920 X

PHOTOGRAPHIC CREDITS

ABPL = Anthony Bannister Photo Library
SIL = Struik Image Library

ABPL/A. Bannister: p18 (bottom left), p24 (top left); ABPL/A. Shah: p6/7, p10 (bottom); ABPL/B. Joubert: p5 (top); ABPL/C. Haagner: p2 (bottom right), p3 (centre), p10 (top), p17 (top), p18 (bottom right); ABPL/D. Balfour: p8 (bottom), p21 (bottom); ABPL/D. Hamman: p23 (bottom right); ABPL/E. Lyons: p18 (top); ABPL/G. Hinde: p2 (top), p8 (top); ABPL/L. Hunter: p3 (top left); ABPL/L. Stanton: p11 (bottom); ABPL/N. Dennis: p14 (top right), p16 (centre), p17 (bottom), p19 (bottom), p24 (bottom left, top right); ABPL/P. Chadwick: p22 (bottom left); D. and S. Balfour: p12/13, p14 (top left); D. Balfour: p19 (top), p22 (bottom right); G. Cubitt: p3 (top right), p4 (top and centre), p15 (bottom left); L. Hes: front cover, p5 (bottom), p8 (centre), p9, p20 (top right), p21 (top right); Photo Access/D. van Smeerdijk: p2 (bottom left), p20 (bottom), p21 (left), p23 (top right); Photo Access/P. de la Harpe: p11 (top); Photo Access/Planet Earth/R. Matthews: p15 (right); Photo Access/T. Carew: p22 (top); R. de la Harpe: p3 (bottom right); SIL/Colour Library: p16 (top); SIL/D. and S. Balfour: back cover, title page, p4 (bottom left); SIL/N. Dennis: p20 (top left), p23 (top left), p24 (bottom right); SIL/P. Pickford: p10 (centre), p16 (bottom); SIL/R. de la Harpe: p14 (bottom).

Africa is a continent of beauty and rich natural variety, its
ecological zones ranging from scorching deserts through to
lofty mountains, dense forests and lush deltas. The open, grassy
plains support a host of magnificent animals, of which the big
cats are perhaps the most awe-inspiring. Over 50 full-colour
photographs depict the power and grandeur of these formidable,
yet graceful hunters. Africa's best known and most exciting
large carnivores are proudly displayed in this souvenir
edition, which also provides a fascinating insight into
the world of the smaller predators.

INDABA
PUBLISHING

ISBN 1-86825-920-X

9 781868 259205